Midnight Confessions

The human experience through words.

Ar. Sakshi Salunke

India | USA | UK

Copyright © Ar. Sakshi Salunke
All Rights Reserved.

This book has been self-published with all reasonable efforts taken to make the material error-free by the author. No part of this book shall be used, reproduced in any manner whatsoever without written permission from the author, except in the case of brief quotations embodied in critical articles and reviews.

The Author of this book is solely responsible and liable for its content including but not limited to the views, representations, descriptions, statements, information, opinions, and references ["Content"]. The Content of this book shall not constitute or be construed or deemed to reflect the opinion or expression of the Publisher or Editor. Neither the Publisher nor Editor endorse or approve the Content of this book or guarantee the reliability, accuracy, or completeness of the Content published herein and do not make any representations or warranties of any kind, express or implied, including but not limited to the implied warranties of merchantability, fitness for a particular purpose.

The Publisher and Editor shall not be liable whatsoever...

Made with ❤ on the BookLeaf Publishing Platform
www.bookleafpub.in
www.bookleafpub.com

Dedication

To my mother, whose poetic dreams took flight in my hands, and whose legacy should continue to soar.
To my father, whose unwavering faith and generous love paved the path for my endeavors.
To Shubhie, my cute spark of inspiration, a whirlwind of imagination who empowers me to be bold, and to thrive.
And to that girl who said "One day I am going to get this published."
This book is a testament to their boundless love — a legacy that will resound in the hearts of those who read these words.

Preface

These are the verses of life-for life.
Inspired from the happenings?
Or from the mis happenings?
I care to say less of it.

More of it to be known by you,
Learned from the wondrous.
Learned from the mundane,
I care to say less of it.

Relate it, if it's beaut,
Leave it, if it's not.
Subjective for those who judge,
I care to say less of it.

A poetess or a poet,
For a healed or a broken.
It's a creation to relate,
I care to say less of it.

Every poem has its own drive,
Love, society, or self- it's all alive.
Where it isn't- must be dead,

For an artist, on it I lead.

Whose life, already as judgmental as it seems,
Will this be another judgment.
Whose life, too precious to play low,
Will this be another preface.

Acknowledgements

To the muses who whispered words in my ear, to the heartbeats that fueled my soul, and to the pages that witnessed my deepest fears and highest hopes - thank you. This collection of poems is a testament to the power of love, the sting of death, the beauty of life, and the unbreakable spirit of empowerment. To those who find solace in these words, I offer my deepest gratitude. May these poems be a reflection of our shared humanity.

1. Loop of Love.

Rebirth of life–
Rebirth of night.
A corset of depth,
Dark and tight.

Twilight dripped bleeding-
Wishing it pours on him.
But set for the meet,
Wore it- seen through nothin'.

Oh! I seek,
Those threads of sane.
For these depths are,
nothing but the Vardian plains.

But for the nonce,
I lied, wore it- only to be seen.
Coincidentally he wore that dawn,
Beguiled, as he was keen.

And yet again, it was evinced that I was seen
For the meadows and fortitude.
So I faded to naught, for another dawn,
Just to start anew with "So long, it's been."

2. Similarly ill-Assorted.

All day-she saw it,
A loud lady, a wind in fall.
Castle above- scant coins beneath,
Existence of love, she saw it all.

He heard it linger,
Her picture in his hall.
Like corals-stagnant river,
Existence of self, he heard it all.

Tell her-tell her not
Her eyes couldn't ease.
Tell him-tell him not,
His heart was ripped.

A modern-day window,
Wee gilded and tall.
For grandeur-just futile,
That heard it all.

3. A guy that I want.

A guy that I want,
Is it something that I need?
As if my life depends on him,
As if he is the only thing I'll read.

A guy that I want,
One which is as soothing as greens.
As if my heart beats for him,
As if he is the only thing I'll feel.

A guy that I want,
One who'll breathe me in.
As if I'm the nectar that gets him peace,
As if I'm the only thing he wants to be seen.

A guy that I want,
Who hears my silence firstly.
As if he knows every rhyme,
Every beat - flow in me.

Will I ever meet this guy that I want,
Rest on him as he wraps around me.
As if I'm the only thing he lives for,
As if, forever mine he'll be.

4. Her moon.

Skies to the sea,
He felt like a prince on his knee.
Gentler than gentle,
Just like a stop by the tree.

He broke the walls,
As if he casted a spell on me.
Similar to what,
Spring did to the cherry tree.

Out of sight,
Just like a mirage indeed.
What a shame!
Still, I imagined you and me.

Even after securing,
Miserably I fell.
Blinded as always,
Still, only him I can see.

Words just like a deep howl,
Requesting to the almighty.
As he is her moon,
Just let him be.

5. Real miss in her real room.

Real miss in her real room,
She doesn't mind to be single.
Unless a breeze rattles her window,
Monsoon and winter start to mingle.

Smell of wet soil, and a cold breeze of fall,
Asks her to share it with him.
Real miss in her real room,
Again, starts searching for the book it seems.

Again, a fictional book and a story of the prince,
One guy kneeled down and day dreaming ever since.

He came with a glass of my favorite coffee,
A gentle peck while leaving for the work.
A beautiful note on her lunch box with a toffy,
And a ring of diamond with a smirk.

Real miss on to the conclusion, seems to be rushing.

Giggling and shy, chaos – now – seems to be hushing.

Real miss in her real room
Opened her book, with the tales of her mind,
She started reading it loud.
"He wants me to read it "one of a kind.

6. Protector's vow.

Set a table for two,
An antique, with a mauve linen.
As she perches with nobility,
With wine and dance in queue.

Dismiss dolorous visions and grey,
Alas! These mundane tables and faces.
"What soul lies within, sir?"-silent
She holds a fragile sway.

I shield my lady– an enigma of wisdom
Wit sharpened, an ethical presence
Oh, her beauty must prevail,
As she walks her own trail.

My pride roars in the gentlest place,
And my courage reigns the mountains.
But oh, what a man it is to be,
Who brings back her solace.

She wrote me, bit by bit- changing into a man-
In her feminine diary.
Oh, her pristine must prevail,
As I am written by a woman.

7. Four days of life.

Only one sight of love was spared,
Yearned and lived.

Then,
It did us – apart,
Death was earned – now four days to live.
A Capulet party – the acorn to the Oak,
Now turned out to be the reason I grieve.

If only I could have known the differences,
I would have learned to fall again.
Only to drink that potion,
Only to revive thy pain.

Thee, having a thorough walk of life,
In the mere one sight of love.
It was still a circle of life,
A complete life – and a white dove.

Two and forty hours – thou escaped away,

Oh lord! For me to be born again.
For me, to learn thy eyes,
To sleep on thy tomb and sway.

8. A distilled genesis.

In between these silences of midnight;
I found a word so fathomable-him.
Word-Unaware of the consequences of;
Being understood to its every dimension.

Entangled into the poetry,
While escaping a word maze.
Ironies of worldly meanings-distil,
As he is the ergophile who'll read it.

Letting the quiet prayer of my pen in book,
One letter -a page at a time,
That banged on my ear drums.
Churning myself – blowing life in it.

Into a book-Alchemy of soul.
One with the poetry inside,
Uttering the missing words about him.
While being understood.

At last, tying the ribbon on the chapter,
Honouring the conclusion of our purpose.

9. Insomniac.

Here it comes again, with eyes wide open,
The last refuge of an insomniac.

It starts when I see the lights losing,
In a Deserted pillow and sand slipping in all directions.

For what should I surrender to sleep?
When I can run miles to the conclusions and back.

I've seen it all, lust, hope, tears, like a worn-out movie,
I've seen time stretching itself to infinity.

Should I seek a chance in that infinity?
To rhymey with the symphony of sighs.

No! lost it to perceptions-makes me see the deeds,
I confront sins which walking world won't.

Stripped naked- like the first breathe - unaware of lights,
You think anybody can handle that? – like a baby's cry.

As more to know, the rhythms of dark – unaware of hope
Hyper aware of light, I saw people brainwashed and robotic.

And here I am, tormented, gave birth every night,
Ink spilling over these mere papers, for them to read it in daylight.

10. It's all in irony.

'I" can never be merged with a "Soul",
For this mere humanly experience.
For this mere run-in loops,
But there's a way to it, in reverse.

Chaos will be understood in silence,
Expose it, and it will chant "Maya".
Unravel these threads of "I", wean from each thread,
And you will knit your bliss.

If you want to be held, then release,
What you've clutched on to, open your palms.
Unravel those lines where fate resides,
Let it flow through those cracks; Maya will slip off.

One neither waits to begin, nor for the end,
Still, one waits for things to help, to walk through.
When its all about gliding, a light leaf on the river,
Separating from the other branches, to the sea of wisdom.

11. Why not to search?

One world, one life – bone and flesh,
Try being a soul – adorned by the destructible.
One breathe, one death – naked ash,
Where one gets stuck - other lives.

Its not complicated or a circle,
Its straight and humble,
It's a boat of slumber – nothing to stumble,
It's a life – which ones gone – nobody remembers.

Help! for I understood to live – while other can't,
Help! For I choose to sleep – while others can't,
Help! For I am not giving in to them,
Help them! For they lost another life in cupidity – while I didn't.

Mortal breath – mortal judgement,
Mortal pieces of hearts with same bone & flesh
One cries for the love – while other over papers,

While the love is in us – burning oneself to the naked ash.

12. So, what if it swept by?

A day swept by- the seconds yet to intertwine.
A day swept by- questioning if I'm losing my mind?

A day swept by- numb and no one even tried,
A day swept by - and yes, we all lied.

A day swept by- now melting overnight,
Looking for the answers that seems out of sight.

Another day swept by, still in this fight.
Heart is all over the place, hold it for a while.

Breathe for a day, laugh as it rise,
Pause for a second, cry for your lies.

Say that it's okay, if you're still reaching the sky.
Breathe honey, it's just a day that swept by.

13. Silence.

Silence – what is it?
A word or a need?
Is it the night after a day weighed in stone?
Or is it the dawn after a one reckless night?

Is it the crowd less summit?
Or a lonely path to it?
I guess it's just one that we feed,
Or may be the one that we need.

Stop! Here comes another dawn,
Don't move! It's another pawn.
Just breathe! Then step on the white,
Pray! And call it a night.

Hear – Reassurance of heart,
Banging on my ear drums.
Feel – Movement of your breathe,
Through your lungs.

Embrace – Light beaming on to-
These healthy eyes every morning.
Let's ask – What is silence?
Is it you or a need.

14. Are you afraid to jump off too?

Are you afraid to jump off too?
Yes, these daydreams are too good to be true.
Scared of how beautiful they might can look?
Exactly! It holds two sides – grey and blue.

Greys for the untravelled path,
And blues for the wide-awake dawns.
All – that isn't even mine,
Yes, I am afraid – to lose it all.

But daydreams are possible,
And yes, they can be true.
As we saw it with open eyes,
And kept it as we grew.

So, am I afraid to jump off too?
Yes, I am but now – there's some work to do.
Let it be a shame of failure but never a pill of regret,
Doesn't matter if I'm afraid to jump off too.

15. Certainly necessary.

Was it necessary to fall? I ask
Was it necessary to risk it all?
How come it looked so beautiful?
Should I live it again, or to escape it all?

I said - yes it was necessary,
To make me feel small.
As I should know my worth,
As I should know the fault.

Yes, the fall was necessary,
For a home without a wall.
Painted by the memories,
Or the rainbow-colored vault.

16. The night when i found home.

A darker night - a beautiful night,
Deeper whispers and a numinous sight.

Wandering without any home but still,
Realised – the hiraeth I feel.

A Death Valley – bellow that lively sky,
A wolf and his moon – a love story or a lie.

A strong rhythm and surroundings asleep,
Sound of howling – pain and separation.

Amazed by metamorphosis,
Morning's love to ironic nights exception.

I saw – sun everywhere,
But here I am – with perdu mysteries to share.

A quick sand – less to move,

Giving up – finally a love to prove.

An eye from the wolf's side,
Saw beaut – a home to hide.

17. Why isn't she gentle?

I saw power – in the kitchen,
When it was tied behind the curtain.
Shaking yet strong- Soon leaving the home,
Liberty over femininity – what a bargain!

I saw power-in the office cabins,
Against a superiors' ugly demands-
When slaps on his cheeks- reddens the sky,
Vigorous over gentle – dragging him to the ends.

I saw power- in the playground,
Her- conquering the game- in a pink uniform.
Father cheering up,
Mindset over barbie- a warrior, a storm.

18. I dare!

I dare! Walked that path alone,
I dare! A tree that's already outgrown.
Play small? Who said to do so,
A sheepish groove walked by the same clown.

Alas! The misery of not waking up bold,
What to do and what not – always being told.
I dare! To command the pride of an overlord,
This dignity is to be worshiped and not to be sold.

God bless your babies – who still feed on sins,
A weakened honour and a snake skin.
I dare! To slit open a cutthroat as I walk away,
Already poured it on their graves with a grin.

I dare! To worship myself, before a man will ever do,
A crown and boots – not your ordinary Cinderella shoe.
Now I dare you to – try to catch and clutch,
A savage liberty will gift you your heart and grave too.

19. Yes I heard him well.

Talk of dignity from a very virtuous man,
And I heard about a woman handicap.
"A beauty tied up with corset strings" he explained.
And I heard about a lamb, waiting for a slap.

"She must wait for my words" he grinned,
And I saw a timorous cry.
"A word of token" I love to give it,
Disguised as a slap of manipulation – an ego so dry.

"Obedient and intelligent"
To hide his own stupidity,
"With all her doors closed"
For him to open his pants in a new city.

Talk of dignity from a very generous man,
And I heard a beg for his esteem – as much as he can.
So as a woman, I dropped it in his bag,
And left him at the sewer – exactly from where he began.

20. Traditions.

Tradition, it's misunderstood and seems fearful now,
Dictator or a guru, blindfolded under sins and vow.
I opened my eyes to look out for my boons,
They told me to close it; it's a cursed eclipse now.

I walked up to them, as I heard about peace,
People and their "saints" were preaching as they please.
So, I came back to the shore for my own leap,
But my legs were tied up – saying that it's a ritual it seems.

I spoke – out loud with a roar, threatened by my sound,
They labelled me "atheist" while I was trying to be found.
It's about peace and not about the differences,
Rituals and traditions look more like a cage and wolves around.

Liberty and devotion are old school now,
Let us bring the business and servants who bow.

Walk up to us only to snatch your visions,
So, nobody should see the truth, as our tradition don't allow.

I call out – those rituals and the mere act of devotion,
A saint outside and, inside drowned in the filthy ocean.
I don't fear death as I know who's almighty,
I clutch the throats of these snakes under the tradition.

21. I saw life, I lived life.

I saw life in,
the brown and dark greens.
Lived, when I learned defying it,
Like a birch tree where lunar hue leans.

I saw life in desert and sands,
Where fear unwinds.
Lived, when I became a mirage,
Peeking on the surface – where hope aligns.

I saw life in the depth of salt waters,
In corals and the creature, it brings.
Lived, while understanding,
The resilience of flush water springs.

I saw life below the soil,
As reds and blacks, a disaster after a stigma.
Lived, when learned to let it out,
Melting into the heat of lava and magma.

I saw life in the sky,
In blues and violets.
Lived it when understood,
Being grounded as mountains.

I saw life from greens to greys,
Understood how to defy it.
Lived, when learnt resilience,
When truly – I never tried to fit.

22. A valley of dead dreams.

A wide-eyed child and a shackle,
A fruit of reaching for the sky.
To a room with only a red window,
A rule-every well must run dry.

An old man with a blinker- glass,
Gives a command- Rip his heart.
"My dreams will die, let your ignorance thaw!"
Heart was ripped, and boy fell apart.

People pulled him out for a carousal,
For being prosaic, the adults who are dead.
Again, silence took over the Hamlet,
Buried stories, that were left unread.

23. I pray it to be.

I fear – that it might feel familiar,
Death – I fear it might not be that scary.
I pray – it to be an experience,
Not a slow slumber – contrary.

I learned life – in chaos,
I will learn death – in intervals.
So, I can see – doves choose violence,
And deserted island with winter birds.

I fear – it to be different from life,
I fear it to be another path of ignorance.
I pray – it to be a string of epiphanies,
It to be like my childhood innocence.

I pray – it to be like,
My mom bringing me back home.
After my first day of school,
It to be her – my hair – and her comb.

I pray – it to be learning to die,
As I learned to live.
I pray – it to be learning to sleep,
As I learned to sew.

I'll than untangle the woven strings of life,
Putting it back in the woollen ball,
Untangling the stories I had while sewing,
Performing my death in an empty hall.

24. She learnt more than just a day.

She wished to run away,
She saw it losing – patience,
Unable to break those thick walls,
To find peace in her own presence.

Neither thought of giving up,
Nor she was tired.
She hustled to have,
That smile she admired.

For her,
Breathing started getting tougher.
Closed room or cold room,
Shivering - nothing to cover.

That day, moon rose with a poetry that,
She thought she'll never understand,
"This body will burn; I mustn't fall"
Midnight wrote the answers on her hand.

She saw hope beaming on,
The tiny dust particles moving around.
Particles as light as nothing,
Can find their own way around.

Somethings seems to be appeared
Only in the hopeful rays.
She learnt something more than,
A cold night or lifeless days.

Survived and moved,
Standing on that ground so lifeless.
She learnt more than just survival,
May be a glamorous night to bless.

25. Serene

A road not taken – a truth,
A clearance of a myth.
I heard callings of the soil,
That wanted to give birth to their first sprout beneath.

A road not taken – a canvas,
It wasn't painted, but found.
Roots were carved on the chest of the forest,
Like a child, when her mother's around.

A road not taken – a sense,
Of looking through the drizzles.
Rays through the drops,
Like a viscous cat and her bristles.

A road not taken – shouldn't be taken,
It preserves the soul,
A chance to the purpose,
Once it's none or a whole.

www.ingramcontent.com/pod-product-compliance
Lightning Source LLC
Chambersburg PA
CBHW070039070426
42449CB00012BA/3098